Interpret Your Dreams

Marcy Schaaf

At night, dreams float like clouds in your mind.

Some dreams are fun, others seem strange or wild.

What could they mean?
Let's explore and find out!

Start by remembering the colors
and scenes.

Was it happy or scary?
How did you feel?

Dreams show feelings you may not notice awake.

Look for patterns or things that often repeat.

A flying dream means you feel free
and light.

Falling dreams might show fear or worry inside.

If you see animals, what could they represent?

Chasing dreams might mean you're avoiding something.

Think of dreams like secret
messages for you.

Your mind uses them to talk in a
different way.

When you wake up, write your dream right away.

Draw pictures of anything you remember clearly.

Ask yourself, what stands out most
in the dream?

Was there a challenge or something to solve?

Dreams can give clues about how to grow strong.

Sometimes, they help you
understand your feelings.

Talking about dreams with
someone can help too.

Each dream is a key to unlock your thoughts.

There's no wrong answer—
dreams belong to you.

Even the weird ones are worth thinking about.

Sometimes, a dream is just a
fun adventure.

Or it could teach you to be brave
and bold.

Take time to listen to what
your dreams say.

They can show you a path or clear
your way.

Your dreams are like stories from deep inside.

With each new dream, explore
with open eyes.

What dream will you explore tonight?

The journey begins when you close
your eyes.

Sweet dreams, little explorer.

Join Our Book of the Month Club!

Looking for the perfect gift that keeps on giving? Join our Book of the Month Club! For just $25 a month, or $250 if you purchase a year upfront, you or your loved ones will receive a handpicked children's book every month, straight to your doorstep.

Here's how it works:
Choose from 15 different languages to receive bilingual books that make learning fun.
Enjoy monthly shipments of our exclusive books that inspire, teach, and entertain children of all ages.
Each month's book is carefully selected to provide a new adventure, valuable lesson, and a chance to explore cultures from around the world.
It's the perfect gift for birthdays, holidays, or just because! Whether you're nurturing a young reader or encouraging language learning, our Book of the Month Club is designed to bring joy to every bookshelf.

Exclusive Bonus: As part of your membership, you'll also receive a monthly podcast about our featured book delivered straight to your email! Listen in for behind-the-scenes insights, fun facts, and tips for making storytime even more magical.

Sign up today at www.Booksbyschaaf.com and start enjoying the gift of reading all year long!

Books By Schaaf

www.BookBySchaaf.com

Find us at: